# CINCINNATI BENGALS

CREATIVE EDUCATION

JOHN NICHOLS

F P
Published by Creative Education
123 South Broad Street, Mankato, Minnesota 56001
Creative Education is an imprint of The Creative Company

Designed by Rita Marshall

Photos by: Allsport USA, AP/Wide World Photos, SportsChrome

**Library of Congress Cataloging-in-Publication Data**

Nichols, John, 1966–
Cincinnati Bengals / by John Nichols.
p. cm. — (NFL today)
Summary: Traces the history of the team from its beginnings through 1999.
ISBN 1-58341-040-6

1. Cincinnati Bengals (Football team)—History—Juvenile literature.
[1. Cincinnati Bengals (Football team)  2. Football—History]  I. Title.
II. Series: NFL today (Mankato, Minn.)

GV956.C54N53          2000
796.332'64'0977178—dc21                                    99-015748

First edition

9  8  7  6  5  4  3  2  1

Cincinnati is known as the "Queen City." Located in the southwest corner of Ohio, Cincinnati is the third-largest city in the state. It is also a major port along the majestic Ohio River, which flows west into the Mississippi.

Despite its nickname, Cincinnati was named not after a queen but a general—Cincinnatus, a famed leader in ancient Rome during the fifth century B.C. The Romans loved athletics, and so does Cincinnati, which was home to the first professional baseball team in the United States, the Cincinnati Reds. The city has always had a love for sports and, since 1968, a love for its pro football team, the Bengals.

*Star cornerback Lemar Parrish.*

In the late 1960s, the American Football League decided to put a team in Cincinnati under Paul Brown's leadership. Brown had been the architect of Ohio's other pro football team, the Cleveland Browns—one of the most successful franchises in the history of the National Football League. In 1962, Brown retired as Cleveland's coach. But when he heard the Bengals were being formed, he jumped at the chance to lead them. Brown became the Bengals' owner, general manager, and coach.

The Bengals weren't a winning team at first, but it didn't take Brown long to make them one. In only its third year of play, Cincinnati won the Central Division of the NFL's American Football Conference. (The NFL and AFL merged in 1970.) The team was loaded with young stars such as running back Essex Johnson, middle linebacker Bill Bergey, defensive tackle Mike Reid, and cornerback Lemar Parrish. The foundation for a championship team was in place, and Brown set out to find a quarterback to take Cincinnati to the top.

**1 9 6 7**

*Paul Brown was named head coach of the Bengals—a position he would hold until 1975.*

## BROWN FINDS HIS QUARTERBACK

**P**aul Brown's choice for the job was Ken Anderson. Few NFL teams had heard of Anderson when he was drafted in 1971 out of tiny Augustana College. Fans wondered how he would adjust to playing in the huge, jam-packed stadiums of the NFL. "As it turned out," Paul Brown said, "it never bothered him a bit because he had been born with poise, and from the start, he looked like a veteran."

By his second year, Anderson was the Bengals' starting quarterback. In his book, *The Paul Brown Story,* the Bengals

*Ferocious linebacker Takeo Spikes.*

**1 9 7 3**

*In his second year as a starter, Ken Anderson passed for 2,428 yards.*

coach compared Anderson to Otto Graham, who had led the Cleveland team to several championships. "Ken ranks just behind Otto Graham as my best quarterback ever. He has all of Otto's physical talents, as well as that one tremendously important attribute for any topflight quarterback—stability."

Led by their talented quarterback, the Bengals won the Central Division title in 1973 and made the playoffs again in 1975. Anderson became known as one of the most accurate passers in pro football. In one game in 1974 against the Pittsburgh Steelers, Anderson picked apart Pittsburgh's "Steel Curtain" defense, completing 20 of 22 passes.

During that 1974 season, Cincinnati tight end Bob Trumpy played the entire year with an injured left elbow. "I couldn't button my shirt, and I couldn't brush my teeth," Trumpy said. "Ken knew about it, and he'd throw to where I could bend my arm and catch it. That's how accurate he was. It was like he was saying, 'I know you can't catch with your left hand, so I'll take care of it.' And he did."

During the mid-1970s, the Bengals were consistent contenders in the AFC Central Division. Anderson had plenty of help on offense, including the sure-handed Trumpy, dangerously fast wide receiver Isaac Curtis, and powerful running back Charles "Boobie" Clark.

## WILLIAMS LEADS BY EXAMPLE

Despite their talent, the Bengals started to fade at the end of the 1970s, becoming one of the worst teams in pro football. Anderson played well, but something was lacking. The Bengals needed a defensive leader. By 1981, the team had found that leader, a man who was as forceful off the field as he was on it. His name was Reggie Williams.

Growing up, Williams wasn't even interested in sports. He wanted to be a good student, but he had a problem—he was born partially deaf. At first, his teachers thought he was a slow learner, and Williams was put in a class with children who had learning problems. Later, several teachers helped him to gradually learn to cope with his hearing impairment.

By the time he reached high school, Williams was a fine student and a sports fan. "As a child, I had very few heroes who let me down," Williams remembered. "Willie Lanier of Kansas City was one of my idols. He was the first black middle linebacker, the 'quarterback of the defense.'"

**1 9 7 5**

*Receiver Isaac Curtis averaged an amazing 21.2 yards per catch.*

Williams went to college at Dartmouth—one of the best schools in the country—and became an outstanding football player. The Bengals drafted him in 1975. Williams would play for the Bengals for 14 years as an outside linebacker.

As talented as Williams was on the field, he was even more important to Cincinnati when he wasn't playing football. He gave much of his free time to charity, including the Cincinnati Speech and Hearing Center for Children. The center was always in need of money, and Williams somehow managed to raise it. "There's always time to demonstrate to other people that you care," Williams said. "And one moment of caring can set in motion a whole series of events that can have a positive impact on somebody's life."

Williams was also having a positive impact on the field. He and fellow linebacker Jim LeClair keyed a defense that became very stingy in 1981. Defensive linemen Ross Browner and Eddie Edwards, along with defensive backs

*Halfback Harold Green, a star of the early '90s.*

*Linebacker Reggie Williams anchored the defense for 14 seasons.*   11

Ken Riley and Louis Breeden, made life miserable for opposing quarterbacks.

What really made the Bengals successful in 1981, though, was the offense. Ken Anderson was named the AFC Player of the Year. He set team records for most yards passing (3,754) and most touchdown passes (29) in a season. In addition, Pete Johnson broke the team's single-season rushing record with 1,077 yards and also scored 16 touchdowns, another Bengals record.

Led by these offensive performances, Cincinnati went 12–4 and won the AFC Central Division. Playoff victories over Buffalo and San Diego put the Bengals in the Super Bowl for the first time. In that game, Cincinnati fell behind San Francisco 20–0 at halftime, but Anderson rallied the team in the second half. With wide receivers Isaac Curtis and Cris Collinsworth well covered, Anderson used tight end Dan Ross to perfection. Ross caught a Super Bowl-record 11 passes as the Bengals scored 21 second-half points. Still, San Francisco held on to win 26–21.

Cincinnati coach Forrest Gregg, who was in only his second year as the Bengals' head man, praised his players. "You guys played one heck of a second half," Gregg said. "Everybody in Cincinnati is proud of you, and you should take pride in yourselves."

Anderson led the Bengals to the playoffs again in 1982, and Williams had his best year ever in 1983, recording 7.5 quarterback sacks and four fumble recoveries. Yet despite these heroics, the Bengals finished with a 7–9 record. After the season, Forrest Gregg left to take the Green Bay Packers head coaching position. Cincinnati's new coach was Sam

**1 9 8 1**

*Bruising fullback Pete Johnson rushed for a total of 1,077 yards.*

Wyche, who had been San Francisco's quarterback coach when the 49ers beat the Bengals in the Super Bowl.

## ESIASON BECOMES A BOOMING SUCCESS

*Ball-hawking cornerback Ken Riley picked off a team-high eight passes.*

**W**yche had been a backup quarterback with the Bengals when the team first began. As a coach with San Francisco, he had helped develop the skills of the great Joe Montana. In his new position in Cincinnati, Wyche would have the opportunity to work with rookie quarterback Boomer Esiason, who was taken by the Bengals in the second round of the 1984 NFL draft.

Esiason came to the Bengals from the University of Maryland with great ability and confidence. His real name was

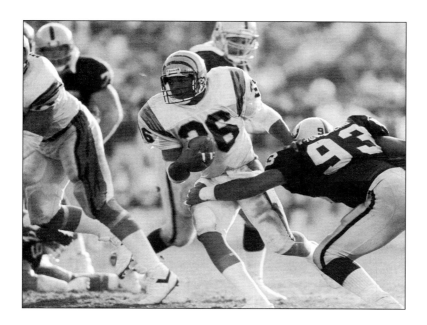

*Cincinnati's leading kick returner, Stanford Jennings.*

*Rookie receiver Tim McGee starred as a kick returner, racking up more than 1,000 yards.*

Norman, but he was nicknamed Boomer by his mother. Boomer had always been a star, but he would struggle in his first few years of pro football.

Anderson, who by then was in his mid-30s, kept Esiason on the bench for a while, but soon Wyche was ready to use his quarterback of the future. Esiason replaced the aging Anderson, and the Bengals began to improve. In 1986, Esiason led Cincinnati to a 10–6 record. The 1987 season, however, was a different story.

Early in the season, the NFL Players Association went on strike. The NFL owners decided they were going to have a season anyway, using what they called "replacement" players. For Esiason, things were particularly difficult. He was the team's union representative, and he supported the strike. Unfortunately, the fans didn't. When the "real" players returned, the fans booed them, especially Esiason. "He was the target of all the hostility that built up among fans during the strike," explained Mike Brown, Cincinnati's assistant general manager. "I don't think I've ever seen one player take the full force of a fan reaction that bad."

The fans booed Esiason, but Wyche never stopped believing in his quarterback. The coach continued to support Esiason even though the Bengals finished 4–11 in 1987. "He's as competitive as any player in the game," Wyche said. "The great thing about Boomer is the way he can sense pressure and slide in the pocket to buy time until his receivers get open. It's a knack."

Esiason and Wyche were both under pressure to produce a winner. The fans wanted owner Paul Brown to fire Wyche after the 1987 season, but Brown wouldn't hear of it. After

*A great Bengals rusher, James Brooks.*

*Anthony Munoz, one of the best offensive tackles of all time.*

this vote of confidence, Wyche knew that the Bengals needed a big season in 1988.

## WOODS SHUFFLES INTO CINCINNATI

*Powerful nose tackle Tim Krumrie emerged as a star, leading the Bengals defense in tackles.*

**W**hen the 1988 Bengals' training camp began, a rookie fullback caught the attention of the Cincinnati coaching staff. Elbert Woods—better known as "Ickey," a nickname from his childhood—ran hard, sometimes flattening his teammates during practice. After one hard-hitting scrimmage, veteran offensive lineman Max Montoya walked up to Woods and said, "If you run the ball like that, you're going to make a lot of money in this league."

"After I said that," Montoya joked, "Ickey's eyes got real big." Woods had dreamed of being an NFL star since childhood, but he grew up in a bad neighborhood in Fresno, California—a neighborhood where kids often turned to crime. "Every night," Woods remembered, "you'd hear ambulances, police sirens, and gunshots." And every night, his mother, Sylvia, would say to him, "You can do better than this."

Woods's football ability earned him a scholarship at the University of Nevada-Las Vegas. At UNLV, Woods and teammate Andre Horn, who was also from Fresno, talked constantly about making it to the professional ranks. Horn would say to Woods, "You know you can make it. I know you can make it. Just hang in there, man. It'll happen."

Woods didn't become a star at UNLV until his senior year. When he finally got his opportunity on the field, Woods showed just how good he was. Off the field, however, Woods had to once more face the bitter realities of his im-

*Boomer Esiason led Cincinnati for 10 seasons (pages 18-19).*

*Tight end Rodney Holman was one of nine Bengals players voted to the Pro Bowl.*

poverished background. His friend Horn had been shot and killed back home in Fresno. The tragedy only intensified Woods's determination to make it in the NFL.

At training camp with the Bengals, Woods showed such talent and hustle that Wyche soon put him in the starting lineup. Led by Woods and Esiason, who was having the best year of any quarterback in the league, the Bengals raced to first place in the AFC Central Division and stayed there throughout the season. The team—but especially Woods—was also entertaining to watch.

The Bengals' star running back had developed a strange dance that he performed after every touchdown he scored. After his teammates gathered around, he hopped a couple of times on one foot, and then hopped a couple of times on the other foot. He finished by shaking his hips. The Cincinnati media started calling it the "Ickey Shuffle." Soon, it seemed everybody was doing the Shuffle. Teammates were doing it. Fans were doing it. Even owner Paul Brown, who was 80 years old, did it once.

Woods gained more than 1,000 yards for the Bengals and scored 18 touchdowns during the 1988 season. As good as Woods was, though, Esiason was better and was named the NFL Offensive Player of the Year. The Bengals' defense was having a great year as well. Reggie Williams, one of the oldest linebackers in the league at age 34, was having one of his best seasons. Nose tackle Tim Krumrie was everywhere, leading the team in tackles.

The Bengals rolled to a 12–4 record and won the AFC Central Division title. They then beat Seattle and Buffalo in the playoffs to advance to the Super Bowl, where they would face San Francisco—the same team that had defeated the Bengals in the 1982 Super Bowl.

Cincinnati started slowly in the big game. The offense could not move the ball, and the defense was having trouble holding down 49ers quarterback Joe Montana. The Bengals suffered a major blow when Krumrie went down in the first quarter with a broken leg. The soul of the defense was gone, but the team didn't lose hope. Despite Montana's heroics, San Francisco managed only a field goal in the first half, and the teams were tied 3–3 after two quarters.

In the second half, Esiason started to connect with his receivers, and Cincinnati took the lead 13–6 on a kickoff return for a touchdown by Stanford Jennings. Montana quickly hit San Francisco's star receiver Jerry Rice for the tying

*Fierce safety David Fulcher led the defense with four interceptions.*

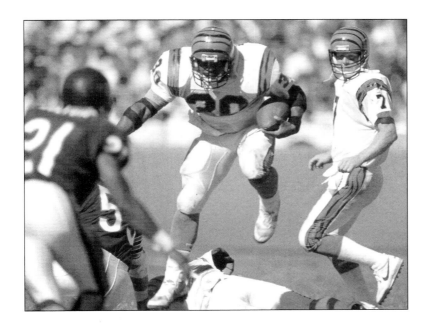

*Charismatic running back Ickey Woods.*

*Sure-handed receiver Cris Collinsworth.*

touchdown. Cincinnati responded with a field goal from Jim Breech, his third of the game. But then Montana broke the Bengals' hearts with a brilliant late-game drive, throwing the winning touchdown with just 34 seconds left. "Thirty-four seconds," Wyche muttered on the sidelines. "We were 34 seconds away." San Francisco won 20–16. The Bengals went home disappointed, but they still believed they had what it took to become NFL champs.

1 9 9 1

*Speedy Eddie Brown led all Bengals receivers with 59 catches and 827 yards.*

Unfortunately, injuries plagued Cincinnati during the 1989 season. Ickey Woods missed almost the whole year after suffering a knee injury in the second game of the season. A sore shoulder bothered Esiason for most of the season, and although Krumrie made an amazing recovery from his broken leg, he wasn't the dominant player he had been in 1988. Despite the injuries, the Bengals finished 8–8 in 1989 and almost made the playoffs.

The team did make the playoffs in 1990, finishing the regular season with a 9–7 record and the AFC Central Division title. Running back James Brooks, who had stepped in for the injured Woods, rushed for more than 1,000 yards for the second consecutive season, while Esiason led a potent passing attack featuring wide receiver Eddie Brown. In the Wild Card game of the playoffs, the Bengals battered the Houston Oilers 41–14. They lost 20–10 to the Los Angeles Raiders in the second round, but hopes were still high for the Bengals to dominate in the 1990s.

Unfortunately, everything then went wrong for Cincinnati, which lost eight straight games the following season. Injuries and declining performances by team veterans took their toll, and Esiason had one of his worst professional seasons, leading the offense to an average of only 16 points per game. The Cincinnati fans and media began to blast both Esiason and Wyche. At the end of the 3–13 season, Bengals management decided to go in a new direction—both at head coach and at quarterback.

## STARTING OVER

*Dave Shula carried on a family tradition as he was named the Bengals' new head coach.*

In 1992, the Bengals replaced Sam Wyche as head coach with Dave Shula. Cincinnati's new head man had strong coaching bloodlines. His father, Don Shula, was the legendary coach of the Miami Dolphins.

In taking control of the Bengals, Shula became the youngest head coach in the NFL. "I'm hoping to bring a new

*Jeff Blake was an accurate passer and swift runner.*

energy to this franchise," said the 32-year-old. "We've got a long way to go, but we're starting fresh today."

The job of rebuilding the Bengals would be a difficult one. The team's stars had begun to age, and it would be Shula's job to replace them. One by one, the impact players of the great Bengals teams of the late 1980s either retired or moved on. One of the biggest losses came with the retirement of left offensive tackle Anthony Munoz after the 1992 season. The mountainous lineman had spent 13 brilliant years in Cincinnati and had firmly established himself as the best tackle of his generation. "Every guy who comes down the pike from now on will have to be compared to Anthony," said Kansas City Chiefs head coach Marty Schottenheimer. "He is the best there ever was."

The loss of the 11-time Pro-Bowler left the Bengals with a gaping hole in their line and a lack of veteran leadership. The youngsters Shula brought in to replace the aging veterans showed great talent, but they lacked the seasoning it takes to make a team a consistent winner in the NFL. Players such as wide receivers Carl Pickens and Darnay Scott and quarterback Jeff Blake sparked the offense, while tackle Dan "Big Daddy" Wilkinson and safety Sam Shade led the defensive charge.

The young team provided fans with many thrills, but the inexperienced Bengals could never quite get over the hump. Growing pains and key injuries seemed to deflate the club on a yearly basis. In 1995, the Bengals selected All-American halfback Ki-Jana Carter from Penn State with the first overall pick in the NFL draft. Carter was considered by many experts to be the best running back to enter the league in

1 9 9 3

*Halfback Harold Green led the team with nearly 600 rushing yards and caught 22 passes.*

*Cincinnati's workhorse halfback, Corey Dillon (pages 26-27).*

25

*Hard-hitting line-backer Brian Simmons led the Bengals defense with 115 tackles.*

many years, and Shula could hardly wait to unleash his new weapon. "Ki-Jana's a franchise-type player," the excited coach explained, "and we will go where he takes us."

Unfortunately, Carter never got the chance. During the Bengals' third preseason game of 1995, the jet-fast halfback took a handoff, pivoted awkwardly to avoid a tackler, and blew out a ligament in his left knee. Carter would miss the entire season, and the Bengals would struggle in yet another losing campaign.

In Shula's four and a half seasons as head coach, Cincinnati managed only a 19–52 record. With the team going nowhere, Shula was replaced as head coach midway through the 1996 season by former Bengals offensive coordinator Bruce Coslet. It was time to rebuild again.

*Fearless wide receiver Carl Pickens.*

In 1997 and 1998, the Bengals continued to be an erratic team. New head coach Bruce Coslet's club could be atrocious one week and brilliant the next. "I'm frustrated by the ups and downs we have experienced," he said, "but right now we are finding out who is going to be a part of the future of this team and who isn't."

One player fans saw as a big step toward a brighter future was quarterback Akili Smith, Cincinnati's first-round pick in the 1999 NFL draft. The 6-foot-2 and 225-pound signal-caller had dazzled NFL scouts by throwing 30 touchdowns and only eight interceptions during his final season at Oregon University in 1998. "Akili brings us a big package of talent," noted Coslet. "He's big, he's fast, and he has a powerful arm. He has all the raw talent in the world. Now it's a matter of teaching him to use it against NFL defenses."

Smith wasn't the team's only reason for optimism, though. The Bengals offense also featured playmakers Carl Pickens and Darnay Scott at wide receiver and big tight end Tony McGee. On defense, Cincinnati was led by a pair of aggressive young linebackers, Takeo Spikes and Brian Simmons. Both were potential stars with great speed and explosive strength. "We've suffered through the growing pains with these kids the last couple of seasons," said Coach Coslet. "Now it's time for them to start to produce."

Unfortunately, that production would not come in 1999. Cincinnati limped through another frustrating season, finishing 4-12. Although the Bengals' final record was a disappointment, Smith managed to give Cincinnati fans a glimpse

**2 0 0 1**

*The Bengals were counting on tackle Willie Anderson to anchor their offensive line.*

*Exciting quarterback Akili Smith.*

*One of the AFC's top receivers, Darnay Scott.*

of his enormous potential. With the Bengals' record at 0–4, Coslet decided to give the strong-armed rookie his first NFL start. Facing the Cleveland Browns on the road, Smith completed 25 of 42 passes, including a game-winning touchdown strike to Carl Pickens with five seconds remaining, to lead the Bengals to an 18–17 win.

Another bright spot for the Bengals was the play of halfback Corey Dillon. He ran for more than 1,100 yards for the third straight season and showed sure hands as a receiver out of the backfield. "Corey's a workhorse," said Coslet. "He's a back who just gets better and better as the game goes along."

The Bengals future should only get brighter as they continue their history in a brand new home—Paul Brown Stadium, a natural-grass facility. With the off-season addition of speedy Florida State wideout Peter Warrick—the fourth overall pick in the 2000 NFL draft—Cincinnati's new generation of heroes appears ready to make its roar heard across the NFL.